Why Is There Evil?

Crucial Questions booklets provide a quick introduction to definitive Christian truths. This expanding collection includes titles such as:

Who Is Jesus?

Can I Trust the Bible?

Does Prayer Change Things?

Can I Know God's Will?

How Should I Live in This World?

What Does It Mean to Be Born Again?

Can I Be Sure I'm Saved?

What Is Faith?

What Can I Do with My Guilt?

What Is the Trinity?

TO BROWSE THE REST OF THE SERIES, PLEASE VISIT: LIGONIER.ORG/CQ

CQ

Why Is There Evil?

R.C. SPROUL

 LIGONIER MINISTRIES

Why Is There Evil?
© 2021 by the R.C. Sproul Trust

Published by Ligonier Ministries
421 Ligonier Court, Sanford, FL 32771
Ligonier.org

Printed in China
RR Donnelley
0000122
First printing

ISBN 978-1-64289-338-0 (Paperback)
ISBN 978-1-64289-339-7 (ePub)
ISBN 978-1-64289-340-3 (Kindle)

Cover design: Ligonier Creative
Interior typeset: Katherine Lloyd, The DESK

Scripture quotations are from the ESV® Bible (The Holy Bible, English Standard Version®), copyright © 2001 by Crossway, a publishing ministry of Good News Publishers. Used by permission. All rights reserved.

Library of Congress Control Number: 2021931271

Contents

Chapter One

The Problem of Evil

Two separate but closely related problems that Christians often hear when people object to Christianity are the problem of evil and the problem of human suffering. The first problem with respect to evil is usually stated like this: How can a being who is infinitely righteous, holy, and perfect create a creation or a creature with even the possibility of sin's being present? If all things go back to the being of God, would we not have to find evil somewhere within God Himself to account for the presence of evil in this world? So the question of evil has to do with the integrity and holiness of God. The question of suffering is closely related, but it is not the same question. The question of suffering is, How can a benevolent God allow all the suffering that we find existing in life? These are two separate questions. The first is more of a philosophical question. The second is more of a practical question of dealing with the problem of pain, anguish, and tragedy in this world. Let's look at one at a time.

A nineteenth-century theologian stated that the problem of evil is the Achilles' heel of the Christian faith. He argued that no satisfactory explanation can be given for the existence of evil. Many skeptics and atheists have stated that if God could not have stopped the entrance of evil into the universe, then He is not omnipotent. If He could have stopped it but chose not to stop it, then He is not benevolent. So either way you look at the problem of evil, somehow a shadow is cast over the nature of God.

Historically, many attempts have been made to answer the question of the origin of evil from a Christian perspective, and those attempts have come to us by means of what is called *theodicy*. A theodicy—from the Greek meaning "to justify God"—is an attempt to justify God for the existence of evil in the world. But in my opinion, no one has yet been able to adequately answer the question of the problem of evil.

The first thing a Christian must do when he's confronted with this question is to immediately say, "I don't know the answer," and acknowledge the seriousness of the question. Don't try to play games. Don't try to hide. Don't try to evade it, but deal with it head-on. It's important that people see that we Christians recognize there's a serious problem here, that we're not oblivious to it. So let's look at a couple theodicies to see how some have dealt with this problem. First, some have approached this question by denying the reality of evil altogether and arguing that evil is an illusion. In my opinion, that's a cop-out, because it does not seriously reckon with the reality that we all experience every day.

The second approach is that evil is actually a necessary prerequisite for the appreciation of the good, and so in the final analysis evil is good. Let's state it in concrete terms: For man to really experience goodness in freedom, he had to experience the problem of evil. He had to experience the reality of evil so that he might appreciate his redemption. In this schema, which has been offered many times in the history of the church, the fall was actually a leap forward. It was a fall upward rather than downward. This fails to deal adequately and seriously with the negative judgment that God Himself placed on the entrance into the world of human sin.

Another important and fascinating theodicy is the one offered by Gottfried Leibniz, who was in the rationalist school of philosophy that grew out of seventeenth-century Cartesian thought. Leibniz's theodicy is clever, and I have seen Christian people use it to convince other people that we do have an explanation for the origin of sin. In fact, I did an experiment once in a philosophy class in college. I told the students that I was going to give them a philosophical explanation for the problem of evil, and I produced Leibniz's case as passionately and eloquently as I could. When I was finished with my lecture, I asked the class, "Does that make sense?" Every single student in that class bought the argument. That taught me something. I realized I could use this argument and win debates all the time. But I knew it was wrong, and I knew there was a fallacious element to it. After I showed the class why they shouldn't have accepted that argument, they changed their minds. But Leibniz's case can be very persuasive, and I warn you that Christian integrity demands that we don't use such sophistry in dealing with the question.

Leibniz begins his theodicy by making a threefold distinction with respect to evil. He distinguishes between what he calls moral evil, physical evil, and metaphysical evil. Evil in all these notions involves a common thread of meaning: in each, evil is defined in negative categories as some kind of lack. This goes back to the medieval definition of evil as *privatio* or privation, a lack of the good.

Moral evil is a lack of moral good. It's a deficiency. Physical evil is a deficiency of physical good. Metaphysical evil is a deficiency of metaphysical goodness. Moral evil has to do with the actions of moral creatures, the volitional behavioral patterns of moral agents. Physical evil would be those things that we describe in terms of calamity or tragedy: earthquakes, tornadoes, fire, wind, storm, and pestilence. Metaphysical evil has to do with ontological imperfection. Ontology concerns "being," the essence of things. An ontological matter is what something is, its being, its essence. Metaphysical imperfection is to be less than an eternal self-existent being, to be less than ultimate. An imperfect thing would be that which is created and dependent, that which undergoes change, generation, and decay. In a word, that which is metaphysically lacking is that which is finite.

Leibniz's basic thesis is that physical evil "flows out of" metaphysical evil, and moral evil "flows out of" physical evil. So, the reason we have moral evil is because the world is full of metaphysically imperfect beings. I sin because I'm weak. I'm weak because I'm finite. And the only way I could be without sin would be if I could transcend the intrinsic metaphysical weakness that associates itself with finite creatures. To err is human, because we're finite. There are limits to our knowledge, our physical strength, and our endurance. By definition, we are not all-powerful, we are not all-wise, we are not all the things that God is. So there is a sense in which it is inevitable that out of my simple human weakness I would sin.

But the question remains, Why would God create such a limited, weak, finite creature? Leibniz understood that the fact that God creates at all is a benevolent act on His part. So we can't fault God for wanting to create. But if God is going to give this gift of life, this gift of being, to other creatures, how can He best do it? Why doesn't He create man morally perfect? This is the judgment the skeptics have raised. If God is going to create man, why doesn't He create him perfectly good?

Leibniz says it's because He can't. Even God cannot create a perfectly good creature, because to create him perfectly good morally, He would also have to create him perfectly good physically, and to create him perfectly good physically, He would have to create him perfectly good metaphysically, and that is impossible, because He would have to create another God. He would have to create another God who is infinite, eternal, self-existent, and complete in His being. But it is impossible for God to create another God. Why? Because whatever God creates would be dependent on the first God for its existence. It would not be eternal. It would not have self-existence. It would be inferior ontologically to the Creator who brought it into being in the first place. The very fact that it had a temporal beginning would differentiate itself from the original God. So God cannot create another God, but God could create an almost infinite number of different kinds of being.

The issue is not, Must God create a perfect world? We can't demand that He create a perfect world. But if God is moral, if He is righteous, we can demand that God create the best of all possible worlds. The hypothetical world that philosophers posit is an impossible situation. The question the philosopher should raise isn't, Why is there evil? Rather, the philosopher should say, "Isn't it nice that God has not created the world with more evil in it than it already has?" He's done the best He can. He has created the best of all possible worlds.

Leibniz's principal adversary was Voltaire. Voltaire's play *Candide* was written to attack Leibniz; the character Dr. Pangloss represents Leibniz. Dr. Pangloss talks about the best of all possible worlds. The Lisbon earthquake hits, and thousands die, and still Pangloss talks about the best of all possible worlds. That was Voltaire's satirical comment against Leibniz's thesis of theodicy.

Now, there are problems with Leibniz's theodicy. There is an intellectual problem and a biblical problem. The intellectual problem is that he has committed one of the most basic errors of reasoning, but it is one of the most difficult kinds of errors of reasoning to discern. He's committed the fallacy of equivocation. In each one of these distinctions, the meaning of the term *evil* changes. Moral evil carries with it the notion of that which deserves punitive measures. Moral evil by definition is the kind of evil that comes out of volitional creatures. Metaphysical evil, on the other hand, excuses man from being morally evil. It offers man and God an excuse. It not only justifies God for the existence of evil, but it also justifies man for the existence of evil. Man cannot really be held responsible because it's necessary for him to sin because of his metaphysical imperfection. And if it's necessary for men to sin, how can we stand in judgment for doing what we must do by nature?

Biblically, we have other problems. First, if this schema is correct, then it would be impossible for us to be free of moral evil in heaven, unless God does more than glorify us; He must deify us to make us free of evil. Second, it means that Adam never falls. Adam was created evil, at least metaphysically evil and physically evil, which excuses him morally. So from many perspectives, Leibniz's argument cannot function as a Christian theodicy for the problem of evil.

Other attempts that have been made to answer the question of evil have been somewhat naive. A standard reply of Christians to the origin of evil is that it originates in man's freedom, and for man to be free, he had to have the capacity to do right or wrong. And so, God gave man the right to choose. He gave him freedom, and to give a creature freedom to choose evil is not to make him evil or to be responsible for that evil. We can therefore locate the origin of evil in the sinful choices of man in his freedom.

Biblically, we can certainly acknowledge that man is free and that man is held accountable and responsible for his sin. But the real question of the origin of evil has not been solved by merely pointing to human freedom. Why not? You still have to ask, Why did that man choose to do evil? And that takes us back to the point of considering the implications of the fall of Adam and Eve. What prompted Adam and Eve to choose evil rather than good? All kinds of answers have been offered to that question. Some say: "The devil made them do it. They were deceived by the deceiver." But the question that immediately comes to mind is, If they sinned out of deception, was it really a sin? Would they not have sinned in excusable ignorance if they really did not know?

The other problem with that argument is that the biblical record tells us Adam and Eve *did* know. God explicitly told them what they were allowed to do and what they were not allowed to do. So we can't understand the entrance of sin into the world as happening by deception. How about by coercion? Suppose the devil forced them to do it? Again, if it were an act of coercion, then God would not hold them responsible. But God does hold them responsible. And the narrative gives us no hint that they were coerced into sinning. Every time we read the narrative, we see Adam and Eve sinning out of an act of choosing, out of a free, voluntary act.

Here's the real question: In what state were Adam and Eve before they sinned, from a moral perspective? What was the inclination of their will? Was the inclination of their will only toward the good, was it only toward the bad, or was it neutral?

When we choose, we always choose according to our strongest inclination, our strongest desire. That's what the essence of choice is: the mind choosing. I do something because that's what I want to do. That's what it means to make a choice. It's an action proceeding from a desire.

Now, if the inclination of Adam and Eve's heart was evil before they made the evil choice, what would be the problem with that? It would mean they were fallen before they fell, that they sinned because they were sinners. It would mean that sin is not the result of Adam's fall, but it's the result of creation. God would have created someone with an evil inclination, and judging from biblical categories, even the inclination toward evil is considered sin by

God. So if we say that they sinned because they had an evil inclination, then they were acting according to their evil nature. That would make God the author of sin, and that's not biblical. But suppose their inclination was only to the good; then how could they possibly have chosen evil? That would not explain their sin. What if their inclination was neutral? What if their inclination was neither to the good or to the evil? Then they would have had no reason for their choice. It would mean they just did it with no moral disposition, one way or the other. It wouldn't even be a moral act. But there's an even bigger philosophical problem. If people have no disposition toward choosing, can they choose? No, the neutral status of the will leaves a person in paralysis. There is no way to choose. So that can't explain it. So what is the Christian left with in terms of explaining the fall?

At this point, we have to ask, Is it a sin to be tempted to do something evil? What if I am tempted to do something sinful, but I choose not to act on the temptation? Have I sinned? I would say it depends on what we mean by *tempted*.

In the garden, the father of lies came along and said it would be fine to eat the fruit. So let's take a look at eating.

To see that something is potentially good, and to consider and desire to eat something that is good and then taste it, is not wrong. Jesus was hungry in the wilderness. There was no problem in Jesus' being hungry and desiring food; there was no sin in that. There would be sin only if He acted on that desire. But if He *desired* to disobey God, that would be a sin. If I sit around desiring to do something that is intrinsically evil, then I've already sinned inwardly. That's where this becomes very complicated. We can see how Adam and Eve would consider the fruit to be beautiful and appetizing and to desire it, but their desire for the food came into conflict with their desire to please God.

We also must consider what it means to be free. The humanistic notion of freedom is the ability to make a choice with no prior disposition, no inclination, nothing that would incline us to a certain direction, so that our choices would be completely unpredictable and spontaneous. If we accept that notion of freedom, then we also accept the philosophical principle that something can come out of nothing.

The issue is determinism versus indeterminism. Freedom is not indeterminacy. Indeterminism is an empty concept. There's no such thing as indeterminism. Everything is determined. The question is, What is the locus of determination? The essence of freedom is self-determination, rather than being determined by something or someone outside myself. Freedom means doing what I want to do. Am I not being free when I do what I want to do? The reason I do it is because I want to do it. That's the cause. I have an inclination to do it. I can say: "My mind approves it. I think it's good. I want to do it." And so I do it. Is that a free act, or has it been determined by my desires? If it's been determined by me, can we say that it's not free? The essence of freedom is self-determination, but it is a kind of determinism; that is, the act is determined by the person making the choice.

Now here we have another problem. When we talk about creation *ex nihilo*, out of nothing, a misunderstanding of that concept runs around our culture today. When Augustine talked about creation *ex nihilo*, he did not say that the world came out of nothing in the absolute sense. He was saying that there was no preexistent matter that God used to shape and form the universe. Certainly the world came out of something; it came out of God, out of the mind or the purposes of God. And why did it come? Because God intended that it should come because He wanted it to come. There's a reason why the creation came.

It didn't just happen; nor did God arbitrarily, capriciously, or spontaneously create the world. He wanted that world to create. It was an intellectual, intelligent decision. He had a desire to create before He created. Yes, even God has to have a desire to do something before He does it. That's the essence of freedom. That's what God is. God is free to do what He wants.

A definition we have to use for freedom is the ability to choose what you want. The ability to choose without any desire is spontaneous generation, and that kind of creation even God cannot do. Even God doesn't have the power of self-creation or spontaneous generation. He has the power to bring something out of nothing materially. But that "out of nothing" does not mean that He didn't have a predisposition to do it.

We cannot simply say that someone acted by free choice. We must ask *why* did someone freely choose that? What inclined him to freely choose that? There's no satisfactory logical explanation for the sin of Adam. When we consider the good, the bad, and the neutral, we have to make a choice out of one of these three, and it has to be a reasoned choice. One might be logically impossible. Another destroys the integrity of God. Another perplexes the greatest minds of history. But the one that the church has always taken is that man's disposition was only to the good, yet he chose evil.

This is a mystery. I don't know how it can be done, but I know that it was done. Karl Barth called it the "impossible possibility." I don't like to call it the "impossible possibility" because if it happened, then it was possible. But we just don't know how it's possible. It is a mystery how man sinned.

However, the fact that it's a mystery today doesn't mean that the answer to our question won't be discovered tomorrow. As my mentor John Gerstner once told me, a brilliant theologian could come along and figure this out. He pointed out that many times in my life as a student I had faced a difficult question that I could not resolve, but then later I resolved the problem.

Does all this mean that when we face critics of the Christian faith who are wrestling with the problem of evil, our only option is to surrender? Do we have to abandon the Christian faith? No, because when we talk about the problem of evil, we must also talk about the problem of *good*.

We know that we face the reality of evil. Now, what are the prerequisites for the problem of evil to even exist? What must there be for evil to be a problem? The good.

There is no ultimate problem of evil unless there is first ultimate goodness. The existence of evil is one of the overwhelming testimonies to the existence of God. That's the irony of this argument: there can't be a problem of evil unless there's first a problem of the good. We always define evil in negative, dependent, derived categories. We recall the medieval distinction that evil was *privatio* or *negatio*— that is, it's a privation or a negation of the good. It's a lack. It's a deficiency. Evil is dependent on good as a standard for its definition. How does the Bible treat the problem of evil? How does the Bible describe evil? Negatively. Unrighteousness, lawlessness, disobedience, immorality, antichrist, and so on. Immorality can only be defined in terms of what morality is. Disobedience can only be judged against the background of what obedience is. The negative needs the positive as a reference point to even exist.

Only if we assume ultimate goodness can evil become a problem. Of course, a philosopher might say that we are assuming the good, but if there is a good, the good is not really good because we have the problem of evil. The philosopher will say we have to eliminate the notion of ultimate goodness and embrace the notion that there is no such thing as good or evil.

That is a weighty response. That's the basic case for nihilism. But most people who argue against the existence of God from a reference point of the problem of evil assume the reality of good. When I speak with people, I grant that I have a problem with the problem of evil. But I tell them my problem is half as big as theirs. If you really think evil exists, then you have a problem of explaining how evil can exist apart from the good. And the only way you can account for ultimate goodness is in God. So your argument drives you to God or to the denial of the reality of evil.

But even after we have explored the problem of evil, we still need to address one of the emotional arguments against the Christian faith: the problem of suffering. We will explore that further in future chapters.

Chapter Two

What Is Evil and Where Did It Come From?

I t would be impossible to fully address the questions "What is evil?" and "Where did it come from?" in one short chapter. But I will attempt a short introduction to these weighty issues.

When we ask, What is evil? we first must understand that we use the verb *is* in different ways. When we try to define evil, we face the issue of whether evil really *is* at all. That might seem strange to us, but my first assertion is that evil *isn't*—that is, it *is not*. Why? Because evil *is nothing*.

The Christian Science religion denies the reality of evil altogether and considers evil to be an illusion. That is not what I am promoting. I once debated a spokesperson for Christian Science on the question of the nature of evil. His position was that evil is an illusion. In the course of our discussion, I asked him if he thought that I was an illusion. He said that he did not think I was an illusion. He considered that I was real. So I asked him, "Do you think it's good that I am saying that evil is not an illusion?" He did not think it was good. I then said, "If it's not good that I'm saying that, then it must be bad, and so here's one example of an evil that is not an illusion."

So what do I mean when I say that evil is nothing? I take the word *nothing* and rest on its etymological derivation, where the term *nothing* comes from the combination of a negative prefix and a subject. The word *nothing* really means "no thing."

I stress this point because in the culture we get the idea that evil is some kind of independent substance, something that is in your drinking water or in the clouds, some independent force or power that exists in and of itself and influences the affairs of your life and of this world. So the first thing we have to say about what evil *is* is what it *is not*. It is not a *thing* that has existence. Evil has no being. It has no ontological status.

Rather, evil is an action of something that is a thing. I am something. You are something. When I do something that is not good, then I am doing something that is evil, but evil then is an activity of some being. It has no being itself. Now that may seem like a pedantic point and of no immediate concern to the second question of where evil comes from, but later I will try to indicate why our definition of evil is so important to the deeper question of where it comes from.

The two great theologian philosophers in the history of the church who have addressed the question of what evil is were Augustine of Hippo and Thomas Aquinas. Both Augustine and Thomas used two Latin words to describe the nature of evil: *negatio* and *privatio*. *Privatio* comes into the English language with the word *privation*, and *negatio* comes into the English language with the word *negation*. So historically and classically, the nature of evil has been defined in terms of negation and privation.

In philosophy and theology, one of the most important

ways that we try to give definitions to things that are mysterious is by using the method called *the way of negation*. This method talks in terms of what something *is not*. For example, when we talk about the character and the being of God, we say that God is infinite. What does that mean? It means He is not finite. That's an application of this way of negation. Augustine and Thomas believed that to discuss the nature of evil, which the Bible calls the mystery of iniquity, we have to first understand it by way of negation, by what it *is not*.

Now, evil in this sense can be defined only against the backdrop of what is good. The Bible defines evil using words such as *ungodliness*, *unrighteousness*, and *injustice*. Each term is used as the negation, the opposite of the positive thing that's being affirmed. Injustice or *un*-justness can be understood only against the previous concept of justice. Unrighteousness can be recognized as *un*righteousness only against the background of righteousness. In this sense, the great theologians would say that evil is like a parasite. It can't be known in and of itself as some independent being but can be known and understood only against the positive standard. And like a parasite, if the host dies, the parasite dies with it, because the parasite depends on the host for its own strength and existence. This is true of evil. We can't really define it except against the background of *the good*.

The other word Augustine and Thomas used is *privation*, which is deficiency. If you don't get something you want, that doesn't mean that you're experiencing deprivation, but if you don't get something that you need, then you can say that you have been deprived, that you are lacking something that is necessary and essential to your very being. The Westminster Standards ask, What is sin? According to the Westminster Shorter Catechism, "Sin is any want of conformity unto, or transgression of, the law of God" (Q&A 14). Confessionally, sin or moral evil is defined in terms of a lack, a privation, a want of conformity to the law of God. Righteousness involves conforming to the law of God, doing what God commands. But sin enters when we fail to do what God commands and we fail to conform to His standards of what is righteous.

The Reformers of the sixteenth century added to the classic definition of evil. They agreed that evil is negation and privation, but lest anyone should conclude that because evil has no being, no independent status, then evil is an illusion, the Reformers added another Latin term: *actuosa*. Evil is *privatio actuosa*, which means that though evil is not something that exists in and of itself, *it is real*, and its effects are devastating. There is an *actual privation*, an activated disobedience to the Word of God. And because real beings act out real evil, though evil is not independent, it is nevertheless real. So that's where we start with the questions "What is evil?" and "Where does it come from?" That's the easy part of the two questions.

The second question has to do with the origin of evil and how evil could intrude into a universe created by a God who is altogether holy and righteous. Not only is this universe created by such a God, but it is also governed and ruled by such a God. If this God is holy and righteous, how can He tolerate so much evil in the world? The origin of evil has been called the Achilles' heel of Christianity. Critics of Christianity have said, "Where the Christian truth claim is most vulnerable is at this point of the presence of evil in a world allegedly made and governed by a good and holy God." Sometimes we Christians fail to feel the weight of that problem.

Philosopher John Stuart Mill said that the presence of evil makes the very existence of God problematic, because in the Christian view of God we say that, on the one hand, God is omnipotent. He possesses all power. On the other hand, we say God is loving and good. Mill looked at the pain and sorrow and suffering and moral evil in this world and said these two ideas, the goodness of God and the omnipotence of God, cannot logically cohere or coexist. His argument was this: If God is all-powerful and has the power to create a universe without evil or has the power to rid the universe of evil at any given moment, but He doesn't do it, then He's not good or loving. What kind of being who has omnipotent power could stand by and observe the pain, suffering, and wickedness in a universe of His own creation and not eliminate it? Therefore, Mill said, He can't be good. If, on the other hand, God is good and loving and wants to abolish the evil that brings so much of a blemish to His creation, but He doesn't do it, that means He is not omnipotent. God is either not good or He is not all-powerful. There is an adequate solution to this, which we will consider. But before we do, I have to give my short answer to the question, Where did evil come from?

I don't know.

What this question demands philosophically and theologically is an adequate theodicy. As we learned in chapter 1, a theodicy is an intellectual, reasoned defense of God for the problem of evil in the universe. In other words, it's an attempt to answer the critique of John Stuart Mill and others and to justify God for this problem of evil. I have studied many theodicies, but not one can completely satisfy.

About once a month, I receive a letter from someone who says he has solved the problem of the origin of evil. The answers I find in these letters are simplistic. People usually don't see the depth of the problem.

The most common answer I receive is that the origin of evil has to be located in human free will. We all understand that the one who brings moral evil into the world is man. It was Adam and Eve, and they were exercising the faculty of choosing, in which they had been endowed by their Creator; they made choices that resulted in evil. Sin came into being because Adam or Eve (or both of them) freely decided to disobey God, just as Lucifer, when he was a good angel, was transformed into an evil fallen angel when he exercised his free will by choosing to disobey God. I do not deny that those choices were made, and I do not deny that they were evil choices. But this explanation does not solve the problem because, as we saw in chapter 1, before choices are made, there has to be some kind of moral inclination. Jonathan Edwards examines this carefully in his classic work *The Freedom of the Will*. He concludes that the only way you can account for an evil choice is by having an evil inclination or disposition to that choice. It's manifest that Adam and Eve's choice was evil, and they chose it according to their will. That's also true of Satan. But the question is, Where did their prior disposition come from? What was it that inclined Adam and Eve to disobey God?

Roman Catholic theology includes the doctrine of *concupiscence*. Rome says that concupiscence, or a strong desire, is *of* sin and *inclines to* sin but is not itself sin. But according to Scripture, that which is of sin and inclines to sin is sinful. A being who has a desire to do something evil, before he chooses to do that evil, is already fallen before he makes the choice.

That's the point many people miss when they say that evil came about because of the free choice of Adam and Eve. But why did these creatures, who were made in the image of God and who were made good, choose to disobey Him? If you say that there was no prior inclination, desire, or disposition, then you've described a choice that is not a moral action at all. You've denied the moral agency of the creature when you say he or she does something arbitrarily.

Some people look at Genesis 3 and conclude that

Adam and Eve were coerced into sinning by the power of Satan. This is the old argument "the devil made me do it." This was the argument Eve gave. It was her theodicy. Adam hitchhiked on that argument when he said to God, "The woman whom you gave to be with me," as if God now had forced evil into Adam through the irresistible power of the wife that God provided for him. Adam essentially said, "Lord, You made her as my helpmate, and she helped me right over the cliff here into the fall." But if evil entered the garden through true demonic coercion, then it would be excusable. And it would not carry the moral judgment that it does carry according to Scripture. It would excuse Adam and Eve because they would have been powerless to resist the temptation of Satan. But not only does that not solve the problem philosophically; it also violates Scripture.

Another argument is based on Satan's being described as the cleverest of all the beasts of the field. He seduces Eve by tricking her with his guileful arguments and fools her, and so Eve falls into sin out of ignorance. Again, if she really had been ignorant with what we call *invincible* ignorance—an ignorance that is impossible to overcome—then she would be guiltless and God would be wicked for punishing her for that act. The appeal to the ignorance of Eve and/or Adam also violates Scripture, because the text tells us that God spoke clearly to Adam and Eve and told them what they must not do and what the consequences would be if they did it. Satan challenges the very premise of God when he says, "Did God actually say, 'You shall not eat of any tree in the garden'?" Now, he knew very well that's not what God had said. But Eve says, "No." Eve becomes the world's first apologist. She defends the integrity of God. "God didn't say that. He said of all the trees of the garden we may freely eat, but then He put this one area out of bounds. He said that if we ate of that, we would surely die." And Satan says, "You will not surely die."

God created Adam and Eve unfallen. Their physical powers were greater than ours because our bodies have been ravaged by the consequences of sin. But not only that, their foolish minds were not darkened because they had not been ruined by original sin, and their ability to think clearly far exceeded any Albert Einstein or Thomas Aquinas or other post-fallen person. If ever a human being would have instantly recognized a violation of the law of noncontradiction, it would have been Eve when the serpent said, "You will not surely die," because she knew that her Creator, to whom she owed her very existence, had said that if they did *A*, then *B* would necessarily follow. Instead, Satan said that if they did *A*, non-*B* would follow. Initially, the serpent was subtle, but then he made a direct assault on the integrity and truthfulness of God. And Eve bought it. But she couldn't appeal to ignorance for her sin. Satan's deception of our human forefathers did not excuse them, because they were morally capable and culpable for recognizing the contradiction to the Word of God and obeying the lie rather than the truth. So the explanation of ignorance falls by its own weight. What are we left with?

As we saw in chapter 1, Swiss theologian Karl Barth called the problem of evil the impossible possibility, which is a contradictory statement. It's a nonsense statement. Barth understood that evil had to be possible, or it couldn't have happened. But we cannot find any way that it was possible. It seems at least on the outside that it was impossible, and yet it happened.

We recall that Gottfried Leibniz argued that we sin because we're finite. He said that metaphysical evil gives rise to physical evil, which brings about moral evil. To err is human, so we have an excuse. Leibniz wasn't the only one who promoted this theodicy. Paul Tillich fell back on Leibniz's argument. Process philosophy uses it. You see it again and again in many different shapes and sizes and forms. Many people tell me that the reason that sin came into the world is because we're finite, and if we are finite, then not only are we prone to sin, but it is inevitable that we do sin. I point out that if sin is a necessary consequence of being finite, then it's excusable. How can God still find fault?

The Bible clearly says that it is a sin to call good evil, and it is a sin to call evil good (Isa. 5:20). And that's a sin we commit every day. When we try to justify our own disobedience and our own moral sinfulness, we try to turn it around and make our evil actually look good. Or when we despise the law of God, which is good, when we say there's something wrong with His law, we are calling good evil. Evil is not good, but it is good that there is evil. Otherwise, evil would not be in a universe ruled by a perfect God. This is a hard statement that is easy to misunderstand.

God has His purpose for the entrance of evil into this world. And in a certain sense, as Augustine said centuries ago, God even ordained that evil come into the world. If He did not ordain it, it wouldn't be here because evil has no power to overcome the sovereign, providential government of this universe. Many Christians love Romans 8:28: "For those who love God all things work together for good, for those who are called according to his purpose." Unless God has sovereign power over evil, He will not be able to keep this promise that we cling to and rely on for encouragement during times of suffering. God is not saying that the bad things we suffer are good things; He says they are *working* for good. God uses them ultimately for good. Unless God has the power over good and evil, He can't make that promise. So for purposes I don't know and I don't understand, God, in a certain sense, ordained that evil come into this world—not naively, so that you may experience the difference between good and evil, but for a redemptive purpose. As Joseph said to his brothers in Genesis 50:20, "As for you, you meant evil against me, but God meant it for good."

That is a hard concept, but if you want to understand it, look at Good Friday. Ultimately, who delivered Jesus up to the gentiles to be killed? Ultimately, who was it who was pleased that He be punished? It pleased the Lord to bruise Him. The blackest act in all of human history is celebrated now by what we call Good Friday. Though the motives and intents of those who were engaged in the trial and the execution of our Lord Jesus Christ, for which they were responsible, were evil, God's sovereign power trumped their evil desires because it was through the foreordination of God that Jesus was crucified. This wasn't an accident in history. God has an ability to order a universe in which He uses evil for perfectly pure and holy purposes, which we will see fully only in glory.

One last point we should remember, which we explored in chapter 1, is that the unbelievers' problem is greatly exacerbated over ours. We have a problem explaining the presence of evil, but again, the only way we can identify something as evil is against the backdrop of the good. Only if good exists does evil become a problem. The presence of evil indirectly points to the reality of the good. It becomes an argument not against God but for the existence of God. The unbeliever not only has to account for the entrance of evil to the world, but he has to account for the existence of good without an author of goodness. He has to say that there is no such thing as evil, and there is no such thing as good. There are only personal preferences. That's what the relativist says, until you steal his wallet; then he suddenly abandons his relativism and says, "That's not right," and he looks for justice.

Though our answer to the question "Where did evil come from?" is essentially "I don't know," it is important to know why this question is such a thorny one and why it is a mystery. Though I don't know or fully understand the origin of evil, I do know the future of it. I do know that it has been overcome and that God will rid this universe of all moral evil, physical evil, and metaphysical evil, as we grow up into the fullness of Christ and inhabit a new heaven and a new earth, where there will be no more crying, no more sin, and no more death.

Chapter Three

Accidents

Years ago my wife was hit in the side of her car by a truck driver at an intersection. We call that an accident. I don't think the truck driver with malice afore-thought intended in his mind to ram into the side of my wife's car with his truck. He didn't mean to do it. And since he didn't mean it, and my wife didn't mean it, and no one else apparently meant it, we call it an accident. But we still have to ask the question, Where was God in all of it? Where was God in the accidents you have experienced in your life?

On September 22, 1993, my wife and I were involved in an unforgettable accident. We were traveling by train from Memphis to Orlando, with a stopover in New Orleans. The previous evening, we boarded a train named the *Sunset Limited* in New Orleans. We entered the last car in the sleeping compartment and retired for the night, comfortable, peaceful, and assuming that on the morrow we would reach our destination and be home.

But everything changed without warning. At three in the morning, I awoke flying through the air, a human projectile experiencing the law of inertia. The train had crashed while it was going seventy miles an hour. Now, when you are in a vehicle that is going seventy miles an hour, and it stops, you continue to go seventy miles an hour. I was in a state of motion. And I was going to stay in motion until something stopped that motion, and what stopped that motion was the wall. I bounced off the wall in the pitch dark amid the screeching noise of metal against metal. I realized we were in the middle of a wreck. But in the intensity of the moment, the first thought that came into my mind was "Is my wife all right?" And she had the same thought about me. We both cried out to each other in the dark, "Are you all right, honey?" She assured me that she was fine and I assured her that I was fine, and then our brief conversation was interrupted by the screams of a woman in the next compartment. She was screaming that she was bleeding and couldn't get out of her room.

The cabin steward banged on my door and on her door, trying to determine how many people were injured. I went into the hallway and helped the cabin steward get the woman's door open. She was not fatally injured, but she was very frightened. At that point, my assumptions changed. When we first crashed, I assumed that we had been involved in an accident at a crossroad, that the train had hit a vehicle. But as I walked down the hall and looked out the window, I saw a gigantic ball of flame rising about seventy-five feet in the air outside my window.

At that point, I thought we must have hit a tanker truck. I still wasn't sure what was going on. We were on the second floor of a double-decker train. People climbed down the stairwell and out the back of the train. We hurried away from the back of the train, away from flames that were coming in our direction. After a few moments, I circled around and came back toward the back of the train to see what was going on. I could see that there was a searchlight of some kind; later I learned it was the searchlight of a boat. The boat had actually caused the accident by hitting the railroad bridge.

Against a backdrop of flame and fog, I could see two train cars in the water. As I stood there and watched, suddenly a ball of fire went through one train car and out the empty end of it, like fire in a funnel. I thought, "If there's anybody still on that car, they have no hope." What I didn't know was that underneath that car was another car submerged on the bottom of the river, where almost no one had survived.

We then sat down on the tracks and huddled with groups of people, a large number of whom had been cast into the water by the train wreck and had managed to swim to shore or were rescued by people on the riverbanks. We all tried to help one another get comfortable as we waited for rescue. But the accident had taken place in the middle of a remote part of Alabama. There was no access to the site by car. There were no roads. The only way in was by rail, and in this case it was a single track, not a double track. The only access was by air or by water.

We began to hear the sounds of a helicopter, but it couldn't land because the flames were so high and intense. A tugboat captain and his crew rescued about seventeen people from the water. But we were told to remain where we were. Finally a train approached us from the rear, and we experienced a sense of "we're going to be rescued."

But the train stopped and just sat, and eventually it backed up and left, and we had no idea why. We later learned that it was a freight train. And when it came upon the accident, it radioed back to Mobile. The people in Mobile already knew from the Coast Guard messages that there had been an accident, but they didn't know the severity of it. They had assembled all their rescue crews in Mobile, prepared the hospitals, gone into their catastrophe alert program, and assembled four hundred rescue people on a train to bring them to the site. But they couldn't bring the train in because the freight train was blocking the tracks. So they had to wait for the freight train to back up all the way to Mobile before they could send the rescue train in. Between the time of the accident and the time the rescue train arrived, three hours had passed.

When the rescue train came, triage was implemented. The most severely injured went to the closest car, and those who were safe and relatively unhurt walked along the sharp rocks of the roadbed and went to the final car on the train. That's what my wife and I did. Vesta and I boarded the last car in the train. I don't know how many people were in that car, but we were the people who were the least injured. We rode to Mobile, which took another hour. And during that time, two passengers on our car had heart attacks from the trauma.

We heard story after story from other passengers about their experiences, but there was no panic. There was no mob violence. People were working together in this situation. We knew that there had to be some fatalities, but nobody knew that this accident was the worst accident in the history of Amtrak, that this accident killed more people than all other fatal incidents in the history of Amtrak combined.

We didn't really realize that until we got to Mobile. The sun was just now coming up, and as we looked out, we saw more than a hundred ambulances gathered to meet us.

Again, more triage took place. We were put on a bus that would take us to the farthest hospital because we were the least injured. Again, it took another hour before we got to that destination. When we arrived in front of the hospital, we were amazed at the number of people there to meet us.

I couldn't help but notice the name of the hospital: Providence Hospital. There we were treated with great tenderness, compassion, and kindness.

When I was finally able to call our family at home, I felt like Peter coming to the door where the people had been praying for him. They shut the door in his face because they thought it was Peter's ghost. When I called, I discovered one of our vice presidents and my son had already left for the airport to fly to Mobile, not knowing whether they were coming for bodies or to bring us home.

We met them at the Mobile airport and returned home. The accident made national news, and I was besieged by newspaper reporters and television people who wanted to interview me.

But when I reflected on everything afterward, the thing that struck me was the questions people asked me. They asked me many silly questions. But the one that they asked most frequently was "Why do you suppose you were so lucky? Why do you think your life was spared and forty-seven other people's lives were taken? Don't you really feel lucky?"

I answered: "No, I don't feel particularly lucky. Maybe I would have been lucky if I had missed the train. But I don't consider these kinds of events matters of luck. I know that my life was in the hands of God."

"But weren't the other people's lives in the hands of God?" I was asked. "Absolutely, they were."

I heard all kinds of stories later. I heard the story of one couple who met some friends in New Orleans. They were in the sleeping car, but their friends did not have a ticket for the sleeping car. And so the couple moved out of the sleeping car and went forward into one of the other cars, and they perished. How lucky is that?

"Why did you live and somebody else didn't?" I was asked. I said: "I don't know. Maybe tomorrow God will take my life. He could have taken it tonight. I know that that night was not my time in the providence of God to die, but it was the time for other people to die." That train rushing at seventy miles an hour, out of control once the bridge collapsed and there was no longer any track for it to run on, was not out of the control of God. The engineer had no control. The tugboat captain had no control. The passengers had no control. But the hand of God was there.

As hard as it is for us to deal with tragedy, it is comforting to know that my life and my death are in God's hands. Somebody asked me, "What did you learn about this theologically?" I said: "I could give you a pious-sounding statement, but I really didn't learn anything because I already knew that my life was in the hands of the providence of God. I already believed in the providence of God before this accident took place. Now, I learned something existentially. I learned something experientially. My doctrine was confirmed through the reality of this situation."

What I found out is that you are never safe. I wasn't safe when I thought I was safe. But I also found out, paradoxically, though not contradictorily, that I am always safe. That is to say, from a human perspective, we are never really safe, but from a divine perspective, if your life is in the hands of God, you are always in a situation of perfect safety. Even those who perished, perished by the hand of God *safely*. My ultimate security and safety do not rest in the plans and provisions I make for this world, but they rest in the provisions of God. And if it's God's provision that my life is to end, I would much rather understand that it's in His hands rather than assume that I am a victim of blind impersonal forces over which neither God nor man has any control.

I don't mean that God reached out from heaven, grabbed that train, and threw it off the bridge and into the water. I don't mean anything as crass as that. But if we believe in God, then we have to believe that the invisible hand of God was sovereignly involved in the Alabama train wreck because God's providence extends where human roads don't. It extends into the night. It extends into the bayou. It extends into the darkness. It extends into the flame. It extends into the wreck. It extends into the wreck of your life, and it extends into every accident you've ever experienced, because we believe that God is a God of providence.

When a child asks, "Why does such and such happen?" we give the brief answer "Because." When we say "because," we are saying that there is something that produced this result. There is a *cause*.

Though there is such a thing as cause and effect in the world, all power ultimately rests with God. God is the supreme cause of everything that comes to pass. He doesn't necessarily do it directly or immediately. He may, and often does, work through causes that are found in this world, but His sovereignty extends over all things, and, ultimately, there is no such thing as an accident.

Now, causes are important for us. We need to know why the grass grows and why the grass dies. We go to doctors to find out what's causing our pain and illness. But we tend to look at secondary causes. The Christian needs to go deeper and look behind the temporal causes of this world and see the invisible hand of God's providence.

Chapter Four

Providence
and Suffering

The Bible teaches that God raises up nations and brings them down. He appoints kings and princes and rulers, and He also scatters them from their thrones. God gave His judgments against Babylon and brought Belshazzar to an ignominious end. But in our own day, we tend to make a dangerous assumption: we assume that God will always be on our side.

During the American Civil War, Christians on both sides were convinced that God was on their side. But in terms of the outcome of the war, it was clear that the Lord was not on both sides because both sides could not win a conflict like that. We remember when President Reagan referred to the Soviet Union during one of the darker moments of the Cold War as an "evil empire." In the Gulf War, Saddam Hussein was often described as satanic or the incarnation of wickedness. We usually assume in the United States that God is on our side. That's dangerous business.

In Old Testament history, God pledged Himself, as a bridegroom pledges himself to a bride, to the people of Israel. Yahweh was the God of Israel. He promised them a manifest destiny. He promised them prosperity. He made a covenant with them, and yet, because of their disobedience, God in His providence sometimes disciplined His own people by bringing chastisement on them by the hands of other nations.

Throughout the book of Judges, when Israel did what was wicked in the sight of the Lord, God would raise up pagan nations to oppress Israel. He used the Philistines, the Midianites, and others as instruments in His own providential hand to bring Israel to repentance. Surely the Babylonian captivity in the Old Testament is viewed as the hand of God executing judgment on His own people. So we must not make the fatal assumption that no matter what we do, God will always fight for us and be on our side.

It's not unthinkable that God would use a wicked nation to exercise His judgment on the United States. When God allowed that to happen to Israel on one occasion in the Old Testament, the prophet Habakkuk struggled desperately with that truth. When the Chaldeans had overrun God's own people, Habakkuk was asking: "How could God allow this to happen? Where is His justice? Where is His benevolence?" He writes: "O Lord, how long shall I cry for help, and you will not hear? Or cry to you, 'Violence!' and you will not save? Why do you make me see iniquity, and why do you idly look at wrong? Destruction and violence are before me; strife and contention arise. So the law is paralyzed, and justice never goes forth. For the wicked surround the righteous; so justice goes forth perverted" (Hab. 1:2–4).

The prophet is saying: "The nation is in shambles. We are oppressed by a foreign power. We are living in days of violence. The law is in obscurity, and those who are righteous feel utterly impotent." An earlier lament from the psalmist asked a similar question: "Why do the wicked prosper and the righteous suffer?" (see Ps. 73). Where is the hand of God in all this? How can He allow this to take place?

Habakkuk continues his complaint when he argues with God: "Are you not from everlasting, O Lᴏʀᴅ my God, my Holy One? We shall not die. O Lᴏʀᴅ, you have ordained them as a judgment, and you, O Rock, have established them for reproof. You who are of purer eyes than to see evil and cannot look at wrong, why do you idly look on traitors and remain silent when the wicked swallows up the man more righteous than he?'" (Hab. 1:12–13).

Habakkuk knew God and understood His character. He knew that God was altogether righteous, that God was perfect in His holiness. And yet Habakkuk said: "God, You are so holy that You can't even look at evil. You can't even stand to behold it, but here it is, and You're not doing anything about it. You are silent, You are inactive, and wickedness and evil are triumphing at every turn." Simply stated, the question that Habakkuk raised is, "Where is God?" The prophet was experiencing a profound sense of the absence of God.

Now, we could rebuke Habakkuk. We could ask if he had read his Bible and knew his history. We could ask whether he knew anything about the ways of God—His long-suffering, patience, and promise to right the scales of justice even though, for a season, injustice may prevail.

But Habakkuk says: "I'm going to go up into my watch-tower, and I'm going to wait, and I'm going to stay there like somebody on a hunger strike. I'm going to remain there and wait, God, until You answer my questions, until You give an appropriate response to this. Because it's not right that a holy God should tolerate this wickedness" (see Hab. 2:1).

That could have been a dangerous position for Habak-kuk to take. If I were to say to God, "I'm going to stand here and demand an answer from You. I don't want You to tolerate wickedness for one more second," God could say to me: "If you don't want Me to tolerate wickedness for one more second, then I'm going to have to annihilate you. You are complaining about My toleration of other people's wickedness, while I am being patient with you." But God didn't say that to Habakkuk.

Instead, God told Habakkuk: "Write the vision; make it plain on tablets, so he may run who reads it. For still the vision awaits its appointed time; it hastens to the end—it will not lie. If it seems slow, wait for it; it will surely come; it will not delay" (Hab. 2:2–3). God is saying: "In

My providence, I appoint the calendar. I set the dates. I manifest My rule in My way and in My time. You don't know when My visitation will take place. But it will come."

God was using the hand of the Chaldeans to chasten His own people. The Chaldeans probably thought that God was on their side. But though for a time God used a nation that was far more wicked than His own people to judge His own people, the Chaldeans would get their judgment in due season.

One thing God promises in His sovereign government of the universe is justice. And that's where we struggle, because in this world we experience and see injustice all the time. We seek justice in the courts, and we're not satisfied with the verdicts of the judges.

When one court decides something, we can appeal to a higher court and try the case again. If we're still not satisfied that justice has prevailed, we can appeal all the way to the Supreme Court. But even then, we understand that the Supreme Court is a misnomer. The Supreme Court of the United States is not the Supreme Court of the universe, and we know that even the Supreme Court of the United States can render verdicts that are unjust.

We ask: "Who will redress this injustice? Who will set

the scales of justice right again?" And God says, "That is My role." He is the Judge of heaven and earth, and He promises judgment; He will set the scales perfectly balanced. Now, we may complain that justice delayed is justice denied. But even in the delay, whatever injustice is found in there, God will redress. That is His promise to us. That is His answer to Habakkuk. He tells the prophet that He has appointed a day, and though it seems slow, the prophet must wait for it, for "it will surely come" (2:3).

The perseverance of the saints is not an abstract doctrine. It is the living out of Christian faith and hope that fundamentally involves trusting God for the future, because there is a future for the people of God. But one of the hardest things in the world is to wait for it. Patience is a virtue. Indeed, it is a fruit of the Spirit of God, without whose assistance we would die in our impatience. But God comes and shows Himself to Habakkuk, who says: "O Lord, I have heard the report of you, and your work, O Lord, do I fear. In the midst of the years revive it; in the midst of the years make it known; in wrath remember mercy" (3:2). Here is a saint praying for revival. I can't think of a text that could possibly be more relevant to our own times than this one.

Then Habakkuk says: "God came . . . the Holy One from Mount Paran. His splendor covered the heavens, and the earth was full of his praise. His brightness was like the light; rays flashed from his hand; and there he veiled his power. Before him went pestilence, and plague followed at his heels. He stood and measured the earth; he looked and shook the nations; then the eternal mountains were scattered" (vv. 3–6).

He then sees the vision of God's hand of judgment falling on the wicked nations. "I hear, and my body trembles; my lips quiver at the sound; rottenness enters into my bones; my legs tremble beneath me" (v. 16).

Sometimes fear strikes us with such intensity and force that our bodies respond involuntary. The body begins to tremble. Habakkuk says, "My lips quiver." Have you ever seen a hurt little child trying hard not to cry, but you know the tears are about to flow and the sobs are about to come because you see the lower lip start to vibrate? It starts to tremble, and you know it's coming. Here's a grown man, his body shaking and trembling and his lips quivering. He says, "Rottenness enters into my bones."

After this experience when Habakkuk meets the living God and has a revival in his own soul, a renewal of his own confidence, and a revitalization of his own faith in divine providence, his book ends in triumph. I think it's one of the most triumphant passages in the entire Old Testament: "Though the fig tree should not blossom, nor fruit be on the vines, the produce of the olive fail and the fields yield no food, the flock be cut off from the fold and there be no herd in the stalls . . ." (v. 17).

Habakkuk lives in an agrarian society with an agrarian economy, and he says, "If all our crops fail, if all of our livestock are slaughtered . . ." That's like saying, "If the Wall Street stock market crashes to the very bottom, if all the industry in the United States turns to rust, if the housing of our nation collapses . . ." Habakkuk says that if everything in which he puts his trust in this world disintegrates, he will "yet . . . rejoice in the LORD; . . . in the God of [his] salvation" (v. 18). That is a man who believes in the providence of God.

Have you ever lived like Habakkuk? Have you ever been frustrated with the events of your life to such a degree that you simply could not understand what God was doing in all of it? Have you ever been angry with God? Have you ever shaken your fist in His face to say, "God, if You're really out there, if You're really righteous, if You're really just, how can You let this happen to me or to my friends?" The tragedies of life, the evil that exists in this world, don't make sense. They don't fit with the holiness of God.

That's what we're reacting to, isn't it? Habakkuk says, "God, You are too holy to even look at inequity, and yet You are watching all this evil taking place all around us, and You're not doing anything about it." But what was the answer? God says that though we think we see clearly, He sees everything more vividly. And He promises that though He is tarrying, in His time and in His way vindication will come to the innocent and punishment will come to the guilty. We simply wait on the Lord. That's the promise of God. That's why we're not to avenge ourselves, because God has promised to make right everything that is not right now.

Chapter Five

Providence
and Evil

God's providence extends over all things—momentous events as well as the minutiae of the world. It extends even over those experiences in this world that, from a human perspective, we define as tragedies or accidents.

We particularly are anguished when we wonder how God's providence relates to the presence of evil. The question of evil casts a shadow over God's benevolence to such a degree that, as we learned in chapter 2, the philosopher John Stuart Mill once remarked that he could not believe in a God who was considered to be both omnipotent and benevolent because God cannot be all-powerful and all-good at the same time. Skeptics assume that the presence of pain and suffering in this world is incompatible with the idea of a good, righteous, benevolent, powerful providence.

We recall that Mill's reasoning went something like this: If God sees suffering and the presence of evil in this world and does not use His power to stop it, then He is not good and loving. If He is loving and good and does not stop it, then He must not be omnipotent.

Harold Kushner wrote about this dilemma in *When Bad Things Happen to Good People*. Kushner allowed the pull of God's omnipotence to be swallowed up by the pull of God's goodness because, in the final analysis, the rabbi gives us a God who cares about the human condition but is powerless to do anything about it. God is at best a divine spectator. He can't do anything more than He has done to alleviate the pain of the human condition.

This is the problem of evil. It's the great philosophical question. The problem of evil deals with imperfections in nature: the violence of storms, floods, and fire. It deals with problems on an international scale, as when Habakkuk questioned why evil nations are able to oppress innocent nations. And it deals with the problem of the individual person who, when confronted with suffering and tragedy, asks: "Why? How could God allow this to happen?"

Scholars and theologians categorize some texts in the Bible as *phrases durae*, or the "hard sayings," the teachings of Jesus that strike us at times as being somewhat harsh. Included in this group of teachings are Jesus' instructions about the final judgment and the reality of hell. That's hard for us. We struggle with these things.

One of those hard sayings is captured for us by Luke: "There were some present at that very time who told [Jesus] about the Galileans whose blood Pilate had mingled with their sacrifices" (Luke 13:1).

An outrageous incident had occurred under the governorship of Pontius Pilate. Roman troops had entered a Jewish sanctuary in Galilee and slaughtered the people who were assembled for worship. And as the sacrifices were being offered on the altar, the blood of the worshiping people was mixed with the blood of bulls and goats. So the people came to Jesus and asked: "What about this, Jesus? You're the great rabbi. You're the great teacher. Explain that for us. How could God allow this travesty to take place, where people who were in the midst of religious devotion could be slaughtered?"

We've seen the same thing happen in our day. We've seen it happen in Israel and in New York City and in Pittsburgh. We may be inclined to bring the same question to Jesus that these people did. "Jesus, where was God? Where was He when Pilate mixed the blood of the Galileans with the sacrifices?"

And what was Jesus' response? Did He say: "I am so very sorry to hear about this. I know that My Father cares very much about protecting you. I've told you that He watches over the lilies of the field and the birds of the air. But the management of this universe, this cosmos, is so demanding that on this particular occasion God overlooked this human event. I will report that to Him and ask Him to be more careful in the future"? Now, you know that is not what Jesus said. Jesus' answer is a hard saying: "Do you think that these Galileans were worse sinners than all the other Galileans, because they suffered in this way?" (v. 2).

Jesus' question raises an important theological question. Does the pain and suffering that we experience in this world have a one-to-one correspondence to the degree of guilt that we bear? When one group of people perish in an accident and others are saved, can we jump to the conclusion that the ones who perished must have been more wicked than the ones who survived?

I was asked that question after the Alabama train wreck. "Why did you survive, R.C., and other people perished?" Did people want me to say that God was pleased with me and He was displeased with those poor souls who died? God forbid that we would come to a conclusion like that. Jesus acknowledges and recognizes that when these tragedies take place, those who suffer may be far more righteous than those who are spared. Jesus is disallowing the supposition that those who perished were worse sinners than all the other Galileans because they suffered such things.

Perhaps we would expect Jesus to continue and say, "I realize there's an injustice here and that God will correct it on the final day," but that's not His conclusion. He looks at the people who are raising the question and says, "No, I tell you; but unless you repent, you will all likewise perish" (v. 5).

At this point, Jesus is answering the objection of John Stuart Mill, who says God cannot be good and at the same time allow human pain and suffering and accidents and tragedies in His universe. Classical Christianity would tell Mill that the reason suffering and pain exist in this world is that God is good, and a good God and a good Judge is not willing to allow evil to go unpunished.

The Bible tells us that we suffer and die ultimately because we sin. That doesn't mean that we suffer in this world in direct proportion to the degree of our guilt and sin. But neither do we suffer as innocent sinless people before almighty God. We must remember the difference between the horizontal plane on which we live in relationship with other people and the vertical plane of our relationship with God. On that horizontal plane, on the plane in which you and I live, I will sometimes treat you unjustly and you will treat me unjustly. You will injure me and I will injure you with no just reason. We have all slandered people, and we have all been slandered by people, but we've never been slandered by God. We have never been falsely accused of anything by God, nor have we ever suffered unjustly at the hand of God.

How do we understand that? What does Jesus mean when He says, "Unless you repent, you will all likewise perish"? Remember that the people who come to Jesus with their question are perplexed because they're surprised by something. They're surprised by suffering. They are astonished that God would allow these things to happen. The focal point of their astonishment is human suffering.

Jesus tells them, and us, that they are asking the wrong question. What should amaze us is that God spares us for any amount of time. What should surprise us is not the manifestation of His justice but the manifestation of His mercy, for unless we repent, we will all likewise perish. The only reason we haven't perished already, Jesus implies, is due not to justice but to mercy.

The assumptions here are simple. The assumptions are that God is holy and just and we are not. Any life we sinners enjoy in the presence of a just and holy God is a life of mercy and grace.

Jesus continues: "No, I tell you; but unless you repent, you will all likewise perish. Or those eighteen on whom the tower in Siloam fell and killed them: do you think that they were worse offenders than all the others who lived in Jerusalem?" (vv. 3–4). People were building a temple in Siloam and, for no reason at all, the temple fell over, and eighteen unfortunate people who were in the path of the falling temple were crushed to death.

Some might say that on that particular afternoon when the temple fell, God was taking a nap. Or He was preoccupied with something else, and His attention was diverted for just a second from that falling tower. But that is not what Jesus said. He gave the same response to the tragedy of the falling temple as He did to the brutality of the action of Pilate's soldiers during the sacrificial slaughter. He says, "No, I tell you; but unless you repent, you will all likewise perish" (v. 5).

One of the most popular hymns in Christendom is "Amazing Grace." I'm not sure it's aptly titled, because when questions like this come up, it is clear that it's not grace that amazes us, but justice. We assume and presume on the patience and mercy and benevolence of God. And when the anvil falls, we have become so accustomed to His grace that we are startled and perplexed, and we become angry, saying, "God, how could You allow this to happen to me?"

Jesus calls us up short at that point. He is tender, concerned, and pastoral. He's not mean and nasty to people in the midst of their pain and suffering. We know how tender He is. Yet on this occasion, He reminds people that we have no previous claim on the mercy of God, and that if suffering befalls us, it is not because God is unrighteous. He has His reason for allowing these things to happen. Though we don't know in every circumstance why God allows these things to happen, the one thing we do know is that God is not being unholy or unrighteous or unjust in allowing the temple to fall.

I know when I'm on my knees before God that I deserve to have every building that I walk past fall on my head. And should the next one fall and crush me to bits, I can only thank God for the grace He has given me and the mercy He has poured out on me so many times in this world.

Grace is not as amazing to us as it should be. We have a tendency as Christians to presume on grace, to think somehow that God is obligated to be gracious to us, and we forget what grace is. By its very definition, grace is voluntary and free; it is not required. If it were required of God to deal with us in a certain way, it would be justice, not grace.

We must get that distinction between justice and grace clear in our minds so that we may understand the graciousness of grace, because grace is the very heart and core of our relationship with God. It's by grace that we live. It's by grace that we live eternally. It is by grace that we are redeemed, and only by grace.

Chapter Six

The Case
of Job

As we have looked at the problem of pain and suffering, we've asked with Habakkuk and with people of the New Testament: "Where is God in all this? How can God allow suffering to take place?"

Many passages throughout Scripture answer these questions to some measure, but the most famous and most extensive biblical response to the problem of pain and suffering is the Old Testament book of Job.

The story begins almost like the first act of a drama.

Scene 1 is in heaven, where Satan the accuser comes before the throne of God. He comes from walking to and fro across the earth, and then he enters the presence of God and mocks Him. Satan says, as it were: "Look down there at this creation. It's a mess. Look at Your creatures that You have made in Your own holy image. They follow me. They walk according to my course. They are faithful and devoted to my laws. I have them in my pocket."

God doesn't debate with Satan. Instead, He says, "Have you considered my servant Job?" (Job 1:8). He is a man of integrity. He is upright. He obeys Me.

Satan's lips begin to drip with cynicism, don't they? "Does Job fear God for no reason?" (v. 9). Come on, God. Sure, Job follows You. Sure, Job obeys You. Certainly, he listens to Your commands. Why shouldn't he? You've made him the wealthiest man in the world. You've given him every single one of his heart's desires. The man prospers in every conceivable way, more than any other person on the face of the earth. God, You've built a hedge around him. You've protected him so much with Your providence, You've blessed him so plentifully by Your providence, that he can't afford to listen to me. But let me at him. Take the hedge down, or just put a door in the hedge. Let me try him. Let me tempt him, and we'll see how long it takes before Your faithful servant begins to follow me and curse You.

That's the challenge. And God agrees to it. He allows Satan to afflict Job in every conceivable way a human being can be afflicted: pain, grief, poverty, disease. But God restricted Satan from taking Job's life. Now, let's read and see what happens to Job.

And the LORD said to Satan, "Behold, all that he has is in your hand. Only against him do not stretch out your hand." So Satan went out from the presence of the LORD.

Now there was a day when his sons and daughters were eating and drinking wine in their oldest brother's house, and there came a messenger to Job and said, "The oxen were plowing and the donkeys feeding beside them, and the Sabeans fell upon them and took them and struck down the servants with the edge of the sword, and I alone have escaped to tell you." While he was yet speaking, there came another and said, "The fire of God fell from heaven and burned up the sheep and the servants and consumed them, and I alone have escaped to tell you." While he was yet speaking, there came another and said, "The Chaldeans formed three groups and made a raid on the camels and took them and struck down the servants with the edge of the sword, and I alone have escaped to tell you." While he was yet speaking, there came another and said, "Your sons and daughters were eating and drinking wine in their oldest brother's house, and behold, a great wind came across the wilderness and struck the four corners of the house, and it fell upon the young people, and they are dead, and I alone have escaped to tell you."

Then Job arose and tore his robe and shaved his head and fell on the ground and worshiped. (vv. 12–20)

That is one of the most incredible statements in all sacred Scripture. The Sabeans took away his livestock, the wind destroyed his family, the Chaldeans stole his camels and killed his servants; every precious possession Job enjoyed was stripped away from him. And he grieved. He tore his garments. He fell to the ground. But when he fell to the ground, he said: "Naked I came from my mother's womb, and naked shall I return. The LORD gave, and the LORD has taken away; blessed be the name of the LORD" (v. 21).

All he had left were his wife and God. His wife had shared in the loss of their children. His wife had shared in the loss of their wealth, livestock, buildings, possessions, and status. And the first woman of Uz now is reduced to sitting next to her husband on a hill of dung, while everyone in the city mocks them. Will she stand by her man? Will she be the helpmate that God had created her to be? Will she bring consolation to her husband when he is afflicted with disease and his flesh begins to rot away? No. She comes to Job and says, "Curse God and die" (2:9). Some people look at these words as those of a loving, affectionate, concerned woman who wants to see her husband's agony end. But what compassionate, kind, and wonderful wife would seek to end the agony of her husband by delivering him to Satan and suggesting that he curse God? "Curse God and die!" But Job replies, "Though he slay me, I will hope in him" (13:15).

Who are the actors in this drama? The characters in this drama include Job, the Chaldeans, the Sabeans, Satan, and God. Whose will is being done? We can imagine hearing the pleas of the Chaldeans and the Sabeans as they stand before God on the last day of judgment. God says: "I remember you Chaldeans. I remember you Sabeans. You're the ones that destroyed Job's livestock, stole his camels, took away his property, and killed his servants. Here is My punishment to you." But they say in their defense: "O God, You can't do that. The devil made us do it. We were just tools in the hands of Satan."

Did the Chaldeans and the Sabeans lose their liberty in this drama? Were they coerced by Satan? Were they not acting as free moral agents when they stole Job's cattle? Of course they were. Satan did not discover some innocent, pure, upright, righteous Sabeans and Chaldeans and then create evil in their hearts to reduce them to puppets in order to make them do his will. No, the Sabeans and the Chaldeans were cattle rustlers from the beginning. They had coveted and lusted after those livestock for years, but they couldn't get through the hedge. They couldn't wait to jump at the opportunity when Satan said, "Let's go get Job."

Now, the intents and choices of the Chaldeans were evil. And Satan's motives were altogether wicked. But it's the other character in the drama whose character we question, and that is God. Can God say on the last day:

"I didn't touch Job. It was Satan who did it. It was the Sabeans or the Chaldeans. I'm innocent of any wrongdoing"? No, God ordained Satan to do this, and the criminal acts of the Sabeans and the Chaldeans were under God's control, providence, and sovereign authority; He allowed it all to happen. We can imagine God saying, "Yes. I did it to manifest My own glory, to stop the mouth of the evil one, and to vindicate the integrity of the man whom Satan had slandered."

God's involvement in this pain and suffering and misery was altogether righteous. But there came a moment when Job himself was not convinced. Job had to listen to the cackling tongues of his "comforters" who came and said to him day after day: "Job, this is your fault. You are suffering only in proportion to the guilt that you bear. God would never allow this to happen to you unless you have some hidden sin from which you are supposed to repent. You are the most miserable of men in your pain because you must be the chief of sinners, and you need to repent."

Job searched his conscience. He essentially said: "Repent of what? Am I so wicked that I don't see what I've done?" Then he begins to shake his fist in the face of God and ask God why. And God doesn't answer. Job gets more and more frustrated and asks again. Then finally, God answers Job. "The LORD answered Job out of the whirlwind and said: 'Who is this who darkens counsel by words without knowledge?'" (Job 38:1).

Do you hear the force of that rebuke? God says to him: "Who is this who darkens counsel with words without knowledge? Watch it, Job! You're casting a shadow over the perfect wisdom of My counsel. You are speaking not from the perspective of omniscience but from the perspective of consummate ignorance. You don't know what you're talking about. And now you've put Me on trial? You want Me to give an answer to your theological questions? You want to interrogate Me? I will answer your questions, but before I answer them, I want you to answer some for Me. Prepare yourself like a man; I will question you, and you shall answer Me. Here's question number one, Job: Where were you when I laid the foundations of the earth?"

He doesn't give Job a chance to respond, but we know the answer to this in Job's mind. "Lord, I wasn't anywhere. I didn't even exist when You laid the foundations of the earth. You are from everlasting to everlasting; I'm not. You are eternal. You are infinite. I'm temporal. I'm finite."

"Answer the question, Job. Who determined the earth's

measurements? Who laid its cornerstone, when the morning stars sang together, and all the sons of God shouted for joy? Who shut the sea in with doors? Who made the clouds and their garments? Who fixed their limits on the skies? Have you commanded the morning since your days began and caused the dawn to know its place?" (see ch. 38).

For two chapters, God interrogates Job. "Can you untie the belt of Orion? Can you draw out the Leviathan with a six-pound test line?" After two and a half chapters of this, God never answers Job's question.

The only way God answers Job's questions is not with an explanation that He has reserved for heaven; He answers it with Himself. And many times that is the only way He answers our questions. This is not an exercise in divine bullying over Job, but it's a crash course on the nature and the character of God. "Job, look at who I am. Job, you can trust Me."

After Job sees this fantastic revelation of God, he says, "I lay my hand on my mouth" (40:4). I will speak no more. I abhor myself, and I repent in dust and ashes. Job realized that in his misery, he lost his head and began to assault the very integrity of God, until God said: "That's enough, Job. Go on back home. You'll find double the camels, double the cows, double the crops, double the children, and double the health. And I will make a hedge around you that will last for eternity."

We can learn many lessons from the marvelous story of Job, such as the lesson of patience in the midst of suffering. But I want us to remember one thing from this brief survey. When we are in pain and groan within our souls as to why afflictions happen, and we come before God—sometimes shaking our fist in His face—we must remember who we are and who He is.

That was the lesson Job had to learn about divine providence; he was not dealing with some kind of naked force or impersonal chance, but he was dealing with a holy God, who is sovereign over everything that takes place in our lives.

Chapter Seven

Suffering
and Sin

The pain and suffering we experience often provoke us to ask, How could God allow these things to happen? We've looked at some important biblical passages that address this question. We considered the plight of the prophet Habakkuk. We looked at the story in the gospel of Luke about the temple of Siloam that fell and crushed eighteen people to death. We looked at the book of Job, the most expansive study of the question of human suffering and pain.

When we ask God why we suffer, another dimension we must grapple with is the relationship between our suffering and our sin.

More than once, a dying person has called me to his or her bedside in order to make a confession. The confessions from the lips of dying people often include deep, dark sins, which they believe are the reason for their suffering and impending death.

A parent of a student once came to the administrator of a Christian school and said, "I don't want my children to be taught that God ever punishes people." The administrator sought my advice. I said: "Well, you better not teach the atonement. You better not teach about the cross. You better not teach about the last judgment. In fact, you better not teach anything about Christianity because you will have to eliminate the righteousness of God, the justice of God, the holiness of God, and the judgment of God." The reality is that God does punish people. Our hope is that He will spare us from that punishment, but we know that if He does punish us, it will be just and holy and righteous.

The universal description of Scripture about the last judgment is that the response of the guilty will be the same. It will be a response of absolute silence. The lips of the convicted will be sealed, not because they have suddenly melted in their hostility toward God, but because they will see in the final tribunal the absolute futility of arguing against the judgment of God. Arguing will be futile, not because we cannot win because of God's power, but because the evidence will be so manifest and the contrast between God's holiness and our sinfulness so vivid that every mouth will be stopped.

An event occurs in the New Testament that speaks to this issue in a most important manner. It's found in the gospel of John: "As [Jesus] passed by, he saw a man blind from birth. And his disciples asked him, 'Rabbi, who sinned, this man or his parents, that he was born blind?'" (9:1–2).

We could comment at great length about this question the disciples are bringing here to Jesus. All we are told is that Jesus was walking down the road when He saw a man who everybody knew was blind, and he had been blind from his birth. We might think that the questions the disciples ask Jesus would go something like this: "Master, there's another blind man. Are You going to touch him? Are You going to heal him? Are You going to restore his sight?" Instead, the disciples look at this blind man in his misery and rather than ask Jesus to do something about the blindness, they make this an occasion for a theological lesson. They say, "Jesus, this man was born blind. Who sinned, the man or his parents, that caused him to be born blind?"

Students of logic know the fallacy of the complex question—a question is posed as an either/or situation when, in fact, there may be other explanations. The disciples assume that there are only two options: this man was born blind because he had committed a sin before he was born or the consequences of the parents' sin had been transferred to the child. A host of theological errors and false assumptions arise with their question, but the question does reveal at least one genuine and sound assumption. The disciples had reduced the possible causes for this man's blindness to two, his own sin or his parents'; they assumed that somebody's sin was responsible for his infirmity.

It's a sound assumption. The Bible teaches repeatedly that it is through sin that death and suffering come into the world. Can we not safely assume that had there been no fall, had there been no sin in the first place, then there would be no pain, suffering, and death in this world? In Eden, no one was blind. When Adam walked through the garden, he didn't have to worry about temples falling down on his head and crushing him or someone mixing his blood with the blood of the sacrifices offered to God. In heaven, there will be no blindness. In heaven, there will be no accidents, no tears, no death, no suffering. Why? Because there will be no sin; there was no pain in Eden because there was no sin.

The Bible also teaches that we are in that sinful condition before we're born, and so we receive some measure of judgment before we have done anything because of our relationship to Adam. The disciples make the proper assumption that somewhere, somehow sin is involved in this man's blindness. But they make a tremendous error when they assume that this man's suffering is a direct, immediate, and proportionate response to his own sin.

Another false assumption the disciples make is that because the parents did something wicked, the child was punished. The Bible does teach that the consequences of sin carry on down through the generations; it does say that God visits the iniquities of His people to the third and fourth generation (see Ex. 34:7). And yet the book of Ezekiel makes it clear that no child is punished directly for a sin that someone else commits. The only time an innocent person has ever suffered for somebody else's sin was on the cross, and that was done voluntarily. Jesus willingly assumed to Himself the sin of His people and bore the pain that it deserved. We cannot cry before God as the people in Ezekiel's day did: "O God, it's not fair. The fathers have eaten sour grapes, and the children's teeth are set on edge" (see Ezek. 18:2).

The disciples err when they assume that there is a direct proportion between the sin the blind man committed and his degree of suffering, or the sin someone else committed and his degree of suffering.

Jesus said that we suffer for reasons other than punishment. The very way of redemption is on the *Via Dolorosa*. Jesus is the Man of Sorrows, intimately acquainted with grief. We are sanctified and draw closer to God through afflictions. Our character is developed, and Jesus' redemptive purposes are such that we will never suffer in vain. The suffering of His people is always redemptive. That is a hard message to believe because when our bodies and hearts ache, we often second-guess the wisdom of God; it doesn't seem redemptive in the moment.

And yet, the Apostles tell us we should not think it is a strange thing when we are visited by affliction because it's in those afflictions that God works His redemption in us (1 Peter 4:12). Though we must endure great tribulation for a season, the Apostle Paul said that the afflictions we bear in the body and in this world are not worthy to be compared with the glory that God has stored up for us in heaven (Rom. 8:18). But when our focus is on our pain, our focus is on the present. All this blind man could see at that moment in his life was nothing—a deep, dark blackness. Presumably, he didn't even know that this discussion was taking place between Jesus and His disciples. He couldn't see them. Maybe his sense of hearing had so developed that he could hear the approach of footsteps and he strained to get some sense of who was coming.

Jesus said: "It was not that this man sinned, or his parents, but that the works of God might be displayed in him. We must work the works of him who sent me while it is day; night is coming, when no one can work. As long as I am in the world, I am the light of the world" (John 9:3–5).

After Jesus answered the theological questions, "he spit on the ground and made mud with the saliva. Then he anointed the man's eyes with the mud and said to him, 'Go, wash in the pool of Siloam.' . . . So he went and washed and came back seeing" (vv. 6–7).

I wonder how long it took him to forget the darkness as

his eyes took in the panorama of people and things before him. He endured his pain for the moment, and for all eternity he has the unimpeded vision of the sweetness of the glory of God.

When we stand before God on judgment day and the books are opened, there will be silence in heaven. That is, we will have nothing to say in our own defense. We will see clearly that all God's works are not only marvelous, but they are altogether just and there is no injustice in His providence. This at times is the hardest thing for Christians to trust, particularly when we see pain, affliction, illness, and death. There, we need to be silent. Yes, we search the Scriptures to learn of His ways, but sometimes the answers don't come, and there is a time and place for a holy silence before the sovereignty of God.

Chapter Eight

Together for Good

One of my favorite trick questions to ask students is "Who was the greatest prophet in the Old Testament?" Seminary students usually answer Isaiah or Jeremiah or Ezekiel or Daniel or whoever happens to be their favorite Old Testament prophet. Then I say, "No, the greatest prophet in the Old Testament was John the Baptist." Jesus says that the Law and the Prophets rule until John—that is, up to and including John.

Another trick question I like is "What negative prohibition does Jesus give more frequently than any other negative prohibition in the New Testament?" The answer is "Fear not." Jesus says it so often that we don't even read it or hear it as a negative prohibition. It almost takes the place of a greeting; when Jesus appears before people, instead of saying hello or shalom, He says: "Don't be afraid. Fear not."

One reason for this is that when Jesus Himself manifested the majesty of God, the awesome, holy, transcendent power that He displayed frightened people. He would have to assuage these fears. He would have to speak to calm people down. But I think He also understood something very basic about us: we are given to fear. We are frightened at many times in our lives.

One of the most frightening things about our lives is the unknown future. We don't know what tomorrow will bring. We don't know if tragedy will befall us at the next turn. We don't know if we'll be stricken with a painful or even terminal disease. And these things frighten us.

How would you feel if Jesus Himself spoke to you today and said: "Don't be afraid. From this moment onward, nothing bad will ever happen to you again"? What would that do for your fears? Wouldn't that put a little extra skip in your step?

In this chapter, I want to consider that in a profound and real sense Jesus has made that commitment already to us. It's an indirect promise, and it's one that we don't always quite grasp in its full implications. And yet, we're familiar enough with this that frequently when polls are taken about people's favorite verses in the New Testament, one particular verse that contains a promise from Christ always makes the list: "And we know that for those who love God all things work together for good, for those who are called according to his purpose" (Rom. 8:28).

It's true that this text doesn't say that only good things happen to God's people. It doesn't say that God will never allow anything bad to happen to us. Those words are not found in the text. I'm inferring something here from the text that I want to examine. The text simply says that God is at work in such a way that all things—that is, everything that we encounter, everything that happens to us, everything that we meet, everything that befalls us— work together for good.

Again, that doesn't mean that everything that happens to us is, when considered in itself, a good thing, but God in His providence is making everything that does happen to us work for our good. So now we have to put our thinking caps on. If everything that happens to us is working for our ultimate good, would it not follow that ultimately everything that happens to us is good? If God is working in it and through it for our good, then we have to say *ultimately* it was good that it happened.

But notice that I am careful to use the qualifier *ultimately*. Now, when we speak in the language of philosophy or theology, we often make a distinction between the *ultimate* and the *proximate*. That distinction, which can be a technical thing, is really a distinction between the remote—that which is far away, out of our immediate vision, out of our immediate grasp—and the near, that which is close at hand and happening in the here and now.

Theologians distinguish between primary and secondary causality when discussing God's providence. We recall the story of Joseph. When he was reunited with his brothers, his brothers were terrified that Joseph would enact vengeance against them. Joseph says to them, "You meant evil against me, but God meant it for good" (Gen. 50:20).

What Joseph is saying is this: "There were two agents involved in my affliction, two causal powers working. It's because of you in this world that I was sold into slavery, thrown into prison, and had to endure so many years of pain and affliction. You were the cause of that."

Yet at the same time in that human causal chain, Joseph recognized that above the actions of his brothers stood the overarching providence of God. Joseph was essentially saying: "You may have caused these things proximately, you may have been the near-at-hand cause, but you were the secondary cause. But I understand that even you do not have the power to sin against me unless it is somehow within the realm of God's overarching providential government of my life. So, ultimately, God's intentions were being worked out, and His intentions were absolutely righteous and good and holy. And He is even able to bring good out of your evil."

That's the fundamental lesson we struggle to understand when we examine the biblical concept of providence. And there is no statement in all Scripture that crystallizes this more exactly or clearly than Romans 8:28.

There are different levels of confidence of belief in the things of God. We may believe in God but still have trouble believing God. We sometimes say: "Lord, I believe. Help my unbelief!" We tend to vacillate; we struggle in the moment of crisis when we are called on to trust the promise of God. Who looks forward to pain? Who looks forward to the death of family members or friends? Who looks forward to wars and all the rest of the evils that befall us in this world?

And when they happen, it is exceedingly difficult to hold firm in our faith and belief that God is at work for good. That's the real test of the Christian life: To what degree are we able to trust God for tomorrow? And yet, it is precisely at the point of our trusting and believing God's promise that these things are working together for our good that is the anecdote to fear.

When I was a little boy, my mother would pray by my bedside at night. She would pray children's prayers that were easy for me to understand, and I had to memorize one that I didn't particularly like. I found it scary: "Now I lay me down to sleep. I pray the Lord my soul to keep. If I should die before I wake, I pray the Lord my soul to take." Every night I went to bed a little bit uncertain whether I was going to wake up in the morning because I had to deal with that idea at nighttime, and I found it frightening.

But another one that she taught was the twenty-third psalm: "The LORD is my shepherd." It's an upbeat psalm.

It's a psalm of trust in the care of divine providence; my life is in the Shepherd's hand. But the part of that prayer that interested me the most were the words "Even though I walk through the valley of the shadow of death, I will fear no evil" (v. 4).

It is one of the hardest truths of God to believe that though I walk through the valley of the shadow of death, I will fear no evil. There are things that lurk in the valley of the shadow of death. There are things in those shadows that frighten me, and I suspect they frighten you. We learned to be afraid of the dark when we were little children, didn't we? And yet the psalmist says that even if he walks in the valley of the shadow of death, he will not be afraid of any evil. Why? "For you are with me" (v. 4)

I once heard an old minister say, "God never promised His people that they would be exempt from walking through the valley of the shadow of death." What God has promised is that when we do go into the valley of the shadow of death, He will go with us.

What would it do for your courage if you really knew that God was there? What if Christ in His incarnate form walked into your home today and said, "This afternoon I want you to go through the valley of the shadow of death, and I'm going to walk there with you"? I know what my response would be. I would say: "Lord, if You're going with me, let's go. What do I have to fear if You're here?" But my fear is that He doesn't really mean it, that maybe as soon as I step foot in that valley, He'll leave.

It's hard to put our trust in the promise of God's presence when we cannot see it. It is said that children orphaned during the Korean War who were staying in safe facilities couldn't sleep at night because of their great fear of starving. Their principal fear was that they wouldn't be able to survive another day because there would be no food. The caregivers started giving each child a piece of bread to hold in his or her hand. The children then were able to sleep in great calmness of spirit because they felt secure with a piece of bread; they had tangible, concrete evidence that their future care was being provided for. This is an example of human providence, but God is saying, "Even if you can't see Me or touch Me, I will be there in the valley of the shadow of death."

When Paul tells us that "all things work together for good," he is not just given to optimism or whistling in the dark; he is teaching us a premise. He is teaching us a law of God that God has promised and committed Himself to.

He guarantees His presence in the midst of suffering, and not only that, He has promised that no matter how things happen to us or what things happen to us in this world, God will redeem them because the God of providence is a redeeming God.

Chapter Nine

Evil Is
Not Good

A danger lurks in our belief that everything that happens to us is *ultimately* good. We can make the fundamental mistake of calling good evil and evil good, something the Bible strictly prohibits. That's the monstrous lie the serpent tells to beguile, tempt, accuse, and seduce God's people away from the truth. We tend to do this in our fallen nature. When we do something that clearly violates God's law, we try to find some way to justify what we have done, some form of rationalization, so that by the time we explain our conduct, it comes out being a virtue rather than a vice, because we call evil good. At the same time, we are accustomed to twisting goodness and evil to such a degree that we will actually call the goodness of God evil.

When the great prophet John the Baptist was thrown into prison, he went through an experience of doubt and struggle. This is the man who stood by the Jordan River and said, "Behold, the Lamb of God, who takes away the sin of the world!" (John 1:29). This is the man who gave his very life for the sake of his testimony to Christ. But while he was in prison, he sent his disciples to Jesus with a question that we might find somewhat troubling. John's disciples asked Jesus, "Are you the one who is to come, or shall we look for another?" (Matt. 11:3). John was walking through the valley of the shadow of death, and he was fearing evil. He was beginning to vacillate in his own faith about the identity of the One whom he had been ordained from birth to declare to be the incarnate presence of God. And he was having a crisis.

How many times have you felt doubt like that? Perhaps you have not just considered the possibility of searching for another Savior or looking for another Redeemer, but you have actually done that. Perhaps you have said, "Christ is not what I'm looking for, so I'm going to see if there's someone else who will do." How did Jesus deal with this inquiry? He said to the disciples of John, "Go and tell John what you hear and see: the blind receive their sight and the lame walk, lepers are cleansed and the deaf hear, and the dead are raised up, and the poor have good news preached to them" (vv. 4–5).

Why did Jesus answer John's inquiry in that manner? Perhaps Jesus was saying something like this: "John, while you're alone and being assaulted with doubts, remember when Satan tempted Me in the wilderness. He wanted Me to do all kinds of things that would move Me out of My vocation. I told him that I could not live by bread alone, but by every word that proceeds forth from the mouth of God. And that word that came from the mouth of God includes Isaiah 61, where the identity and the person and the work of the Messiah is spelled out in detail: 'The Spirit of the Lord GOD is upon me, because the LORD has anointed me to bring good news to the poor; . . . to proclaim liberty to the captives, . . . to proclaim the year of the LORD's favor.'"

In other words, "John, go back and read the job description for the One who is to come, because I'm doing exactly what I'm supposed to do and what the Bible said I would do." But what was the problem? While John was in prison, his expectations of Jesus were not being met. And when his expectations were not being met, doubt about Christ came into his mind.

Now a curious thing happens after John's disciples leave the presence of Jesus. Jesus turns to the people and begins to give testimony not about Himself but about John the Baptist. He said: "What did you go out into the wilderness to see? A reed shaken by the wind?" (v. 7). We wonder why Jesus said that. If people had overheard the conversation between Jesus and John's disciples, perhaps their confidence in John the Baptist was now lessened. So Jesus asked them who they went out in the wilderness to see. Someone dressed in soft clothes? Those who are dressed in soft clothes live in royal palaces. This John, who was languishing in prison because of his testimony about Jesus, is not a reed shaken in the wind. "Among those born of women there has arisen no one greater than John the Baptist" (v. 11).

Then Jesus gives a special beatitude for John: "Blessed is the one who is not offended by me" (v. 6). I think Jesus was thinking about a common idea that we find in Scripture: the concept of the rock of offense, the stone of stumbling. Jesus knew that some people found Him offensive. As

Peter later said, "This Jesus is the stone that was rejected by you, the builders, which has become the cornerstone" (Acts 4:11). And yet, many saw Him as a stumbling block and were offended by Him.

Human relationships sometimes end in dispute and conflict, and people get offended. You offend someone, and you are offended by someone. This is part of the fabric of our daily lives, isn't it? The Bible warns us not to be offensive in our behavior, particularly toward the weak and the little ones. "Woe to the one through whom [temptations to sin] come," Jesus says (Luke 17:1). We are called to be inoffensive in our behavior, but in the field of ethics, we make the distinction between an offense *given* and an offense *taken*. We see this reflected in our language when we say things like "Don't take offense with what I'm about to say. I don't want you to be offended. I don't want to do anything wrong to you. If I really do something that is wrong to you, you have every right to be offended, because I have committed an offense." This concerns an offense *given*.

But sometimes people are offended even when we don't do anything wrong to them. This is the case of the offense *taken*. There was no offense given, yet someone still took offense at what you said or did. A perfect example of this problem focuses on the life of Jesus. If Jesus ever gave an offense unjustly, that would have been a sin, and He would have been no longer sinless. If He's not sinless, He can't save anyone. He can't even save Himself. His sinlessness is an absolute requirement for His qualifying to be our Redeemer. But can we say that no one that ever encountered Jesus was offended? All kinds of people took offense at Jesus. The Pharisees were offended by Jesus. The scribes were offended by Jesus.

Even in this discussion that Jesus is having with the people after He dismisses the disciples of John the Baptist, He says: "To what shall I compare this generation? It is like children sitting in the marketplaces and calling to their playmates, 'We played the flute for you, and you did not dance; we sang a dirge, and you did not mourn'" (Matt. 11:16–17). Jesus is essentially saying, "You people can't be pleased." John came out of the wilderness dressed in bizarre clothing reminiscent of Elijah, living on wild locusts and honey. He told the people to repent, for the kingdom of God is at hand, and they were not ready for it. And what did the Pharisees and scribes say about John the Baptist? They said he had a demon.

Jesus told the scribes and the Pharisees that though they

would not submit to God's command through John the Baptist to be baptized, the common people saw the righteousness of God in him, and they went to the River Jordan and asked to be baptized for cleansing so that they would not be filthy when the bridegroom came.

When John came out of the wilderness, he was doing what was right. And most of the people saw John's actions as good. But others, like the Pharisees and the scribes, saw John's behavior as evil, and they called him a demon. They were calling good evil. They were taking offense at righteousness. Jesus pointed out that John came as an ascetic, a person of intense self-denial living in the wilderness, living on locusts and wild honey. Then Jesus came not fasting, and they accused Him of being a drunkard and a glutton, of eating with tax collectors and evil people. They said Jesus was wicked. Jesus told them they were like the children who, when the flute is played, refuse to dance, and when the dirge is played, refuse to mourn. When John came, it was time for the dirge. The land was in mourning. The people were still in anguish, waiting for their redemption. The wedding hadn't taken place yet. The groom hadn't yet come.

Jesus later taught His disciples that when the bridegroom comes and the wedding is taking place, that is not the time for fasting; that's the time for joy and celebration. When the flute plays, it's time to dance. You don't mourn when the flute plays or dance at the funeral during the dirge.

Now, the very thing John struggled with—and we struggle with—is disappointment in our expectations. If I expect something from you and I don't get it, I am disappointed. I may be even offended. And if you are offended and hurt, your offense may be utterly gratuitous. You have no right to be offended because your expectation was not correct in the first place. If I promise that I'm going to do something by a certain time and I don't do it, however, then you have every right to take offense. This is what John the Baptist was struggling with. While he was in his cell, he thought: "When is Jesus going to make His move? I expected that long before now this One whom I've announced as King would manifest His kingship and drive the Romans out." Jesus wasn't meeting John's expectation. John took offense. "Shall we look for another?" (v. 3).

That's what we do with the providence of God. We have expectations of God, and when He doesn't meet our expectations, we are offended and we start looking for someone who will meet our expectations. This happens because we don't pay attention to what God promises. He says, "I will do every single thing that I have ever promised to do when, in My judgment, it is the appropriate time to do it. If you expect Me to do it when *you* want Me to do it, you're going to be disappointed and you're going to take offense, and you're going to call good evil." But God doesn't do evil, and we must be careful that our faith in the providence of God really is faith that He is working all things together for good for those who love Him and who are called according to His purpose.

Chapter Ten

For Those Who Love God

Perhaps the most famous passage of Scripture that gives us comfort about divine providence is Romans 8:28: "And we know that for those who love God all things work together for good, for those who are called according to his purpose."

In this chapter, we will consider some of the important qualifiers in this verse. All things work together for good for *those who love God* and for *those who are called according to his purpose*. This verse is not a blanket, universal promise from the mouth of God, as if God said, "I'm going to make everything that ever happens work together for the good and the benefit of everyone to whom it happens or by whom it happens." There's a restriction in this promise. The promise is given for those *who love God*.

If you don't love God, then there is no guarantee that everything that happens to you is ultimately for your good. If you are not numbered among those who are called according to God's purpose, if you are actively working against the purposes of God, then you must not take refuge in this verse. The providence of God is a two-edged sword. God's providence includes His government, and God's execution of His government includes His execution of justice. And in His justice, He will punish impenitent sinners.

That is a scary thought. Indeed, it is the scariest of all possible thoughts. It's the one thought that no unbeliever ever wants to think. A person who refuses to submit to God trusts and hopes that God will capriciously, whimsically forgive everything the person ever does and never call the person into account. Our culture finds punishment for crime more and more repulsive. If there is an outcry in this world against the punishments rendered by human governments, how much more is there a protest against any idea that God might punish us?

But God is not interested in being politically correct. God has decreed the punishment of evil. Scripture tells us that He has set a day on which He will judge the whole world, on which He will call every human being to account. If those people do not love God, the supposed good things that they have received from God's hand during their lifetime will actually work against them.

Scripture tells us that the most basic, fundamental, and foundational sin of the human heart is the sin of ingratitude. When Paul tells us in Romans 1:18 that God's wrath is revealed from heaven, he says that His wrath is not revealed against innocence or righteousness or goodness. God is not a tyrant. He's not capricious. Rather, His wrath is revealed against ungodliness and unrighteousness. The most basic, ungodly thing we do as His creatures is, as Paul says, to "not honor him as God or give thanks to him" (v. 21).

First, do you honor God? Do you have a sense of reverence and devotion and affection for the God who made you? According to Paul, God has made His presence known clearly and manifestly; He has already revealed His existence to you (v. 19). All of us in our fallen, corrupt human nature repress that knowledge; we fight against it and seek to flee from it, and we end up refusing to honor God in our minds.

Second, do you have a sense of gratitude toward God? Perhaps you have been personally offended when you made a sacrifice of some sort for another human being. Say you give them something costly or do something good for them, and then you realize that person has absolutely no appreciation for what you've done. He or she displays no gratitude and has no sense of being grateful for your gift. You would find that offensive.

It's also offensive to God, because the Scriptures tell us that every good and perfect gift that we have ever received in this world comes to us from God—everything (James 1:17). You may think that you have earned and deserved every single benefit you've ever received and that you can take the credit for it. You don't take into account that whatever skill or gifts you have were bestowed upon you by your Creator. You insult Him by calling your success either a matter of your own skill or, even worse, a matter of luck. You have despised the benefits of God.

Every time God gives us a gift and is gracious to us, it can become an occasion for the increase of our sin. Every time we receive a gift from God but refuse to acknowledge that it comes from God and refuse to express gratitude to God for it, we become guilty of the sin of ingratitude.

We have already explored that, in light of Romans 8:28, any bad thing that ever takes place in your life ultimately is a good thing. But there's another aspect to that, another face on that coin. If you do not love God, then every good thing that has ever happened to you is ultimately a bad thing, because it is working now toward your destruction. You have hardened your heart and increased your hostility to Him, and with every gift that He gives you, your guilt is multiplied as long as you refuse to be grateful.

Simply put, Romans 8:28 teaches that for those who love God, there is no such thing ultimately as a tragedy. And for those who despise God, there is no such thing ultimately as a blessing. If you don't love God, your blessing will be your curse, and if you do love Him, your curse will be your blessing. There are no other alternatives.

I had a seminary professor who made a distinction not only between good and bad but also between good-good and good-bad, and bad-good and bad-bad. He used that distinction to express what we've been exploring with respect to Romans 8:28. A good-bad thing is something that, humanly speaking, is really a bad thing. My sin is really bad, and I don't want to make the mistake of calling my sin good. It is bad.

When my professor said it's good-bad, he meant that it is bad with respect to what I did. We think of Joseph's brothers, who did something evil to Joseph and it really was evil—and they were held accountable by God for that evil. But God's providence working through that bad brought good. Another example is Judas. Judas' treachery was real treachery; it was real evil. We don't want to say that his evil was good. But it certainly is good that he committed it, because through his treason came the atonement.

On the other hand we have the bad-good. Bad-good is when something good happens to you that works together for your judgment, where the outcome is bad. An example is when we despise the gifts of God, all things work together for our bad. Every blessing to the impenitent person becomes a tragedy. Every good and perfect gift that God bestows upon him ultimately heaps piles of coal on his head because his ingratitude and his injustice toward God are increasingly multiplied. This person is treasuring up wrath against the day of wrath (Rom. 2:5).

We have a foolish propensity not only to believe that

God will not punish us but also to hedge our bets by saying, "If He does punish us, all of our sins are equally serious, and there will be no difference in the punishment."

Men have said to me: "Well, I lusted after that woman. I may as well go ahead and commit adultery. I won't be any more guilty than I already am, and even if there is punishment, it's all the same." Paul said that every single time we refuse to be grateful for the gift of God, that ingratitude goes into a bank account, into a treasury. It is not the treasury of merit; it is not the treasury of the riches of Christ; it is not the treasury of blessing. It is the treasury of wrath. Paul said, "You are storing up wrath for yourself on the day of wrath."

Some hope and pray that there is no such thing as a day of wrath. But if the Old Testament prophets taught anything, they taught that there is an appointed day of wrath. If Jesus ever taught anything, He emphasized the chilling truth that there will be a day of judgment and that every idle word we speak will be brought into account. We might hope that God has no wrath, but He does have wrath. We might hope that there will be no day of wrath, but there is a day of wrath. And if God is capable of wrath and has appointed a day of wrath, the worst thing that we could possibly do is to pile it up, storing up wrath for the day of wrath, which the Bible says will be a day of darkness with no light in it (Amos 5:18).

So we see that Romans 8:28 is good news and it is bad news. For those who love God, who are called according to His purpose and who rejoice in His providential government, it's the best of all possible news. For those who remain ungrateful and unloving toward God, it's the worst of all possible news. What kind of news is it for you?

I firmly believe that the Christian's understanding of divine providence is crucial for how we live the Christian life. My prayer is that every believer comes to a deeper understanding of God and His providential control over all things, including evil.

About the Author

Dr. R.C. Sproul was founder of Ligonier Ministries, founding pastor of Saint Andrew's Chapel in Sanford, Fla., first president of Reformation Bible College, and executive editor of *Tabletalk* magazine. His radio program, *Renewing Your Mind*, is still broadcast daily on hundreds of radio stations around the world and can also be heard online. He was author of more than one hundred books, including *The Holiness of God*, *Chosen by God*, and *Everyone's a Theologian*. He was recognized throughout the world for his articulate defense of the inerrancy of Scripture and the need for God's people to stand with conviction upon His Word.

Free eBooks *by* R.C. Sproul

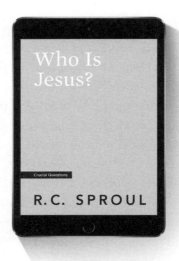

Does prayer really change things? Can I be sure I'm saved? Dr. R.C. Sproul answers these important questions, along with more than thirty others, in his Crucial Questions series. Designed for the Christian or thoughtful inquirer, these booklets can be used for personal study, small groups, and conversations with family and friends. Browse the collection and download your free digital ebooks today.

 Ligonier.org/freeCQ

Get 3 free months
of *Tabletalk*

In 1977, R.C. Sproul started *Tabletalk* magazine.
Today it has become the most widely read subscriber-based monthly
devotional magazine in the world. **Try it free for 3 months.**

TryTabletalk.com/CQ | 800-435-4343

ASK LIGONIER

Do we have free will?

Is it true that God controls everything?

Does prayer change things?

A Place to Find Answers

Maybe you're leading a Bible study tomorrow. Maybe you're just beginning to dig deeper. It's good to know that you can always ask Ligonier. For more than fifty years, Christians have been looking to Ligonier Ministries, the teaching fellowship of R.C. Sproul, for clear and helpful answers to biblical and theological questions. Now you can ask those questions online as they arise, confident that our team will work quickly to provide clear, concise, and trustworthy answers. The *Ask Ligonier* podcast provides another avenue for you to submit questions to some of the most trusted pastors and teachers who are serving the church today. When you have questions, just ask Ligonier.

FOR MORE INFORMATION, VISIT ASK.LIGONIER.ORG